Chronicles of A Poet

By Dr. Allana Todman-Da Graca

Chronicles of A Poet

The author represents and warrants that she either owns or has the legal right to publish all material in this book.

http://drallanadagraca.com

Chronicles of A Poet

Also by Dr. Allana Todman-Da Graca

Tomorrow Can't Wait: Offering Persistence for A Life time Kindle

Tomorrow Can't Wait: Offering Persistence for A Lifetime

Women Build Confidence Coaching in Five Weeks

Social Media & Digital Technology E-Course

I Lost My Job Now What E-Course

Women Build Confidence Coaching Series E-Course

Communication E-courses

LinkedIn Pulse Blog

Dr. Allana Da Graca Self-Development Blog

Http://drallanadagraca.com

It has taken many years for me to find my place of truth. I hope you are able to find a gleam of hope through these poems.

Contents

Chronicles

Hidden gems of my truth

15 years of silence

15 years of Writing

My Dracula

Overwhelmed

Astonished

Hidden

A familiar place 2 be

Recreated

Stagnant Peach

Holding the vase of Resentment

Depression for the blooms

Colloquium dialogue

No transparency

Staring into my Well

Reflection

Missing the Dreamer

Missing Ideology

Missing my MOMENT

15 years

5475 days of **REGRET**

525,600 minutes of **DOUBT**

788,400 minutes of **RESENTMENT**

All because

THEY

Told ME to be _NORMAL_
I MARRIED the concept

In closets I became a

Write-A-Holic

Telling the secrets

Unveiling my Truths

Welcoming New Mystery

INDEPENDENCE DAY

Do you know what it is like to already be dead?

To the point where a gunshot to the head wouldn't do damage,

because your soul and spirit is already gone?

Do you know what it is like when your world halts and everything around you is like a slow motion carousel?

You have an outer body experience and you're almost not even

here, but you carry out the motions of the day

There are many people who walk around dead

Their life squelched by the rivers of pain

Their emotions vanished and the gleam of
their eyes became

faint

Waiting to be found

But still not discovered

The void is consistent as each heart beat

They do not run to a man, or a female, but
to their natural

abilities

They have been so hurt that a brick wall
encases the soul

And they live in an internal jail cell

Some people survive, and others who die
physically were dead

long before

A few people take a hammer and try to
break the wall down

They start pounding away the pain, and the traumatic incident

Friends or family cannot supersede the conviction to live

The brick wall for some comes tumbling down

For others if not early enough,

They die a silent death.

How many mourners will it take to end the recycle of pain?

Broken Glass

If I can find some pieces of glass

I can get on the bus

Ching-A-Ling

Hop on bus #32

Dang

No money today

Search

Like

A

Mouse

Ching-A-Ling

Hands into fist

Doors Open

Ching-A-Ling

Sorry Bus Driver

I

Only

Have

glass

Sidonia's Secrets

Please return to this box

No

Will Not

Please return to this Box

I wish I could

Please return to this box

My pain is hidden there

Please return to this box

I cannot take part in the lie

Enigma Mirrors

Sally was sitting under a shade

She was scared to come out

No one wanted to sit with her at the lunch table

She said.......

Perhaps I am not wearing the right outfit

My copper tone is not pecan enough for any attention

I will just sit under the tree

I will just sit in the shade and write my destiny

I will write about my future

The future is me because I want to be a
doctor

The future is me because I am going to be a
singer

But she stared at her cotton hair

Her fingers clasped the naps and she
prayed for a perm

Perhaps we can think about the little boy

The football players would pounce on

his journey was abuse

He received his beating like rocky without
the gloves

But.......... In the back he was working logic
to scientific projects

But .... No one would ever know
because

He never addressed his personal
scientific truth

You see the Means and sum totals were always negative in his life

And even though he spoke proper English with proper diction He was still

taunted

He was still Picked on

He was still Kicked in the knees

because he was so Smart

The others

Did not understand

They reverted their friendship for jealousy

He laid on the floor.......... closed eyes

His *letter* said

I need to know if you still love me

I need to know if someone still cares

I need to know if someone is listening

I need to know if this even matters

I need to know if anyone cares

And We **say**

How many failures can we accept?

How many dropouts can we tolerate?

What we **fail** to deal with will **deal** with us

Thorns

Wounds on my knees

Scabs of my fears

Beauty of my Findings

The Boulder

All

Worth

It

Re-arrange

Grab

Release

Now

I can

FEEL

FOR ALL THE I DON'TS

I don't have the money

My assignment still stands

I don't have the resources

My creator will make provision for me

I don't have tomorrow

I will plant seeds today

I don't have the sideline encouragers

My angels are my staff

I don't fear when I know I can step beyond the extreme

120 DAYS

What would You do with 120 days?

You've been trying to see things through

What would You with 120 days?

See the life I had before was full of
uncertainty

Clogged like puss formed in a broken hair
follicle

Vague like a blurry vision of Michelangelo's
greatest work

Crushed like a smoothie without syrup

Broken like a shattered piece of glass on a
carpet

Squeamish

Like a Snake slithering through

My Past, Present, Future

Contained like cookies in a cookie jar

Hidden on a countertop away from reach

Sloppy like ketchup on a white shirt

Hidden like a black marker

On a black portrait, on a black wall, in a black hole

Forgotten like gristle on a steak

Useless like a baby's diaper

Tired like the eyes of a 96-year old

Tired like the jacket of a drowned victim

Silenced like a muzzle on a lion

In the back under the table

overly apologetic

Like a crack addict

Addicted to a Behavior that is

Addicted to the **pain** inflicted

By an afflicted person whose inflection was
infected with integrated images

from prior individual incantations of pain

covered in **fits** of outward manifestation

Projected on this being

Stuck like butter on a cheese croissant

Moving one foot forward and the other left in
1982

Inch by inch

Row by row but no current in my river to float

In the middle of the titanic

With no score for my movie

Shattered by what could have been

Grieving all that was lost

Looking at life through a kaleidoscope

of

Fear, resentment and misperception

Holding this voice back in silence

To respect lies

Letting lies outweigh truth

Respecting lies

Consuming lies

Holding my truth to respect the family of fear

But this consistent wandering has allowed me
to hit a Boulder

A boulder has been hit

A boulder that would forever shake my world

It is the Big in my Big Bang Theory

It cracked open truth

A beam of fire in my in my inmost being
cracked through the pain

Of a mask that to the world looked like
success

It said

I KNOW YOUR EXPERIENCE

I KNOW YOUR STORY

I KNOW YOUR PAIN

I SAW YOUR TEARS

I KNOW WHEN YOU WANTED TO END IT

I KNOW THE ABANDONMENT

I KNOW THE ISOLATION

I KNOW THE LOSS

I KNOW THE STORY

I KNOW THE HARDSHIP

I KNOW THE POOR CHOICES

I KNOW A LIFE OF PAIN

I ALSO KNOW

IT IS NOT OVER

IT IS NOT OVER

CAN YOU LIVE DRASTICALLY DIFFERENT?

WHAT WOULD HAPPEN IF YOU HAD 120 DAYS?

Could you

Live DRASTICALLY DIFFERENT?

WHAT WOULD HAPPEN IF YOU CUT OLD TIES?

WHAT WOULD HAPPEN IF YOU DID SOMETHING THIS YEAR?

WHAT WOULD HAPPEN IF YOUR YES WAS YES AND NO WAS NO?

WHAT WOULD HAPPEN IF YOU LET TRUTH REIGN?

WHAT WOULD HAPPEN IF YOU FORGIVE LIFE'S HARDSHIPS?

WHAT WOULD HAPPE IF YOU RECEIVED REDEMPTION FOR ALL THE YEARS Lost?

WHAT WOULD HAPPEN IF YOU ONLY HAD 120 DAYS?

EMPOWERMENT

With open eyes your mountain is there

You stand erect and look to the star's glare

Remember the light within yearns to expand

Set your foot firmly

Commit to a plan

Nothing to lose

You're on your way

Boldly move forward

Dream Today!

QUEEN

I am a Royal Queen

Beyond Beauty

Beyond Intellect

My Aura resonates

A Candle

My spiritual scent

Draws

Many to Admire

Eminence firmly rooted

A Jewel uniquely designed

Processed by my creator

Purpose

That's only

Divine

now

I am victorious

Not because of who I will be tomorrow

My being is firm today

This very minute forming

Lights my path for sure

I am not questioning

My moment in the seconds passing

I am proclaiming my peace

Bonita

You are beautiful

No matter what anyone says

I hear your cry

I hear your sigh

I know you want to be ok

And nothing can hold you back from
meeting destiny

Nothing can hold you down

I hear your cry

I hear your sigh

I hear all the naysayers have been picking
on you

This is your time

To own your life

This is your time

Your season to be strong

I hear your cry

I hear your sigh

This is the moment to live your destiny

You are all that you need

To make your life better

You are all that you need

To make your life strong

Fourth Wind

See the winds captivate my breadth

Circle around three x's

+ one

Looking for a corner to grasp the past

The winds remind me

Transition is underlying

The first wind is knocked down

I was a vagrant collecting heart food from the wrong store

Yeah that first wind it

Knocked me down

told me not to **think**

Of getting down

I assumed the position

Fist ready to punch any enemy

Even the ones I hadn't met

Numbing

My **existence**

Knocking out my spirit

Tying the lips that told me to **trust**

The **second** wind

Rolled me over and I blinked

I thought love opened a new seed

Not realizing my wounds would still bleed

Causing me to frustrate **attention** for love

I longed for laughter living without loss

Arms holding me

would still pay **too much** of a cost

third wind

simultaneously fused the first and second
wind

Saying

Don't try

Stop

Look at you

I knocked you with these winds

Stop trying

When are you going to adjust?

You can live only for today

This message

has been

Interrupted

In a moment you will hear a beep for thirty
seconds

Beep

Beep

Beep

There is no one more faithful

Faithful to feel the flaws of failure

And fear

Forcing flares of flames

Lies felt early

I can observe this **fourth wind**

It consumes me

It's the filling in my cavity

bridge over waters

The Ring in my binder

The Back to my earring

The Saran for my wrap

The tic and tac

The Cover to my pot

The Glue to my transparency

Fourth wind is

Fourth wind has

I think I have been swept

I LOVE YOU

I love you

I love you

I love you

What would I do without **YOU**?

I love you

I love you

I love you

I love you

Stop!

I love you

I love you

I love you

I love you

Thanks!

I love you

I love you

I love you

I love you

How Much Do We OWE?

I love you

I love you

I love you

I love you

I can't wait to get HOME

I love you

I love you

I love you

I love you

What did you say?

I love you

I love you

I love you

I love you

Has it been 9 years?

I love you

I love you

I love you

I love you

I can't stand when you do that!

I love you

I love you

I love you

I love you

Let me be Me!

I love you

I love you

I love you

I can't LIVE without you

I love you

I love you

I love you

Awwwww You are so SWEET

I

LOVE

YOU

Behind This Window

The glass divided between them

Hope and desire

No exchange

No embrace

Freedom seemed more real to the other

Freedom cannot be found

It is

She Knew Their Eyes Met: Sidonia's Chronicles

She looked at her phone and recognized
the first and last name of a male figure

An image accompanied the picture and
reminded her of the loss

A man she was told was still living but
chose to be dead to her

She stared at this image on her phone

The phone number was reminiscent of all of
the hugs and messages she never received

Scrolling through updates of the past

Her thoughts echoed disbelief that her moment of birth was as boring as lint on a used shirt

It was odd to peer in and see this man standing with a brand new family

He had nicknames for his adoptees and it was striking

For every hug he gave his adoptee

she felt a slap of rejection

She closed her eyes and remembered

A glass window between them

She watched his movie play and he maintained his role

He would turn back and look at her glazing at him from the window

He put his head down and looked the other way

She stood there with tears dripping on her shirt

She looked at him through the glass n

She knew their eyes met

Mind Bootcamp

Bootcamp of the mind

Looking to escape

Can you hear me calling?

Bags in circular position

Surrounding the gateways to my soul

How Can I tell you where I am?

Walks like flour milk

Cannot nourish

Intolerant

Going through motions

No Judgement

You have your *M&M's* to choose from

Can I Make It?

Will

i

be

ok?

World gains Teredity

Tiredity

Life+Pressure=Tiredity

After Tiredity and Heredity

What comes next?

Calligraphy

Detailed Lines of passion

Never ending circles of happiness

Looking to be clay

A chance to be MOLDED

Masked

Orphan

Four people in a frame

Four humans with smiles

3 people in a picture

2 people with smiles

1 person in a picture

Without a SMILE

No one is REALLY in the
PICTURE

Yet the **fram**e still hangs

OUT OF THE SHADE

Desire beckons you to move from the rock

The leaves cry out

The sand surrounds your feet

The air slaps your face

You feel out of breadth

No one can hear you cry

No one is asking you why

No one can observe your time

They're still waiting for you to hear them whine

Hours of dedication

To hear someone else speak

No me time

People I serve and seek

No wonder my inner is on a spiritual swerve

It's my time to come out

It's my time to be selfish

My nerves are quickened and I feel anxious

I have no more time to waste

I've had too much patience and haste

"Girl, by and by, just wait on the Lord."

I've waited so long my faith is bored

I know it didn't come in a day

Welded emotions

I need to steal Away

Closer than before but my eyes are blurry

Cold inside like a winter flurry

Spring is here

I will hold out my hand

Reminding myself that I need to

Steal Away

GET UP!

It takes delayed gratification

For me to get your attention

Times spent with angered eyes watered

Nerves asking questions

Unanswered dreams yearn to be massaged

No day spa can rid this tension

Longing to see visions take root

The seed for the sewer had no foundation

Perception

Deceit and vanity took the seed dream

Energy drained

Hope in the wind and lather is none

Yet this taken away from you has been the
pivotal best

Your zeal is on fire

Time has just been re-added

I am reminding you to re-build

The problem is not when you fall

It's when you don't get up

AFFIRMATION OF A SURVIVOR

I am delivered from scattered thinking

My Yes will be Yes and

No will be No

I will not be cowardly unsettled

By situations family or friends

Especially when it comes to my life

I will Love my hair

My skin

My full lips

My feet to stand

My cheeks of splendor

Your Best is in me

I know you are the Creator

I will never be with Lack

I will never wrestle after consulting you

But be planted like a rock

This moment is my life source

All things of yesterday, today and future
are a part of your plan

for my life

There is no more tomorrow

You have changed me today

Close ones who remind me of my past have
no place in my

newness

I must give myself room to detach from
amongst them

Especially when they cannot see the height
you are calling me to

I am a new creature

Though at times I have fallen

I continually stand

You are the **Lord** of my life

About The Author

Dr. Allana Todman-Da Graca, is the founder of Turning On the Lights Global Institute. She has served hundreds of students as a Professor for Lesley University, Allied University, Kaplan U, and Walden University. Dr. Todman- Da Graca has a Doctorate in Education (Capella U), and a Master's in New Media from Emerson College. She has a passion for helping learners persist in their personal and professional lives. In addition to this, she has a love for helping women and teen girls build confidence. She has created online courses (Women Build Confidence, Public Speaking, Social Media and Digital Learning) to help individuals reach their goals by any Creative means necessary.

Made in the USA
Charleston, SC
25 February 2017